Because
The Dawn Breaks!

Poems Dedicated to the Grenadian People.

by Merle Collins

Introduction by
Ngũgĩ Wa Thiong'o

Karia Press

Because the Dawn Breaks
Poems Dedicated to the Grenadian People.

First published in 1985 by **Karia Press.**
Copyright © Merle Collins, 1985.
Copyright © Introduction Ngũgĩ Wa Thiong'o, 1985.

Front cover illustration by Fyna Dowe.
Back cover photograph by Lance Watson.

Cover design by Buzz Johnson.
Book design and layout by Buzz Johnson.
Typeset by Karia.

ISBN 0 946918 08 2 Pb.
ISBN 0 946918 09 0 Hb.

Karia Press
BCM Karia
London WC1N 3XX
United Kingdom

Contents

Introduction by
Ngũgĩ Wa Thiong'o

It is right and appropriate that this collection of poetry
is dedicated to the Grenadian people. For the poems —
their tone, language, content and vibrant commitment
– belong first and foremost to Grenada: the beauty of
her landscape; the challenges of her history; and the
grandeur of her people. So in the poems one hears not
just the voice of Merle Collins, but that of the people
of Grenada talking about their struggles, and in particu-
lar about their five years' experience of revolution and
revolutionary transformation. The poems embody, and
celebrate, the people's visions, dreams and hopes during
those momentous years of hovering on the brink of
tremblingly new and full eternity. And above all is the
celebration of beauty — the beauty of the *new* emerging
from the *old*. I remember, says the poet, the form of the
past foretelling the shape of things to come.

What is that past? It is one of slavery and coloni-
alism and what goes with them: the exploitation, the
oppression, the deformation of spirit. Blackness is
denied: Africanism is denied; the very landscape of
Grenada becomes a matter of shame. Blackness, African-
ness, lower class origins reflected in a mirror become,
particularly for the petty bourgeois educated, a threat
to the self-esteem of those 'caught in the strange dilemma
of non-belonging'. The history celebrated in books and
the media is that of the colonial conquerors. Gairyism
perpetuated this and more. The meek, the exploited and
the oppressed, were supposed to wait for compensation
in heaven. Blessed are the meek. Deliverance will come
from the big houses on the hill!

But that very past is one of continuous resistance
by the meek, Fanon's wretched of the earth, for whom
'struggle is the loudest song'. It was out of that fierce
and continuous struggle that came the 1979 Grenada
Revolution. Merle Collins' poetry captures in telling

images and clear languages the new horizons, the new
possibilities opened up by the revolution. The poem
Callaloo has already become a classic testament of what
the revolution meant at a collective and very personal
level.

> An' wid you head in de air
> becus' de world is yours
> an' you know is yours
> an' you not goin' be
> meek
> meek
> meek
> an' wait to see
> if
> somebody
> goin' let you
> inherit the earth
> becus' you know already
> is yours
>
> So you say
> Loud
> an' clear
> an' proud
> GRENADA!

The revolution reclaims the Grenadian landscape as in
the poem *Magnetic* in which the poetess, returning to
Grenada, is so filled with love that she feels foolish and
strong with pride:

Home again
My land
Home once again
The magnet land . . .

Watch those birds
Watch that land
Watch that sea

Watch them
All together . . .

The revolution reclaims the grandeur of the history of
Grenadian people in *The Lesson*:

And now
We
Consciously
Anti-colonial
Understanding all dat
And a little more
Will cherish
Grannie's memory
And beckon William across
To meet and revere
Our martyrs
Fedon
And Toussaint
And Marryshow
And Tubal Uriah Buzz
Butler
And the countries
And principles
They fought for.

The revolution in fact reclaims for Grenada a new
internationalism beginning with a pan-Caribbean iden-
tity and extending to all the genuine anti-imperialist
struggles of people in Nicaragua, Zimbabwe, Angola,
Mozambique, say Africa, Asia and Latin America.
Revolutionary Grenada then comes to mean,

a country in the Caribbean
in Latin America
in the Americas
in the struggle
in the world

Dat mean, Comrade
a people

> like de people
> in Cuba
> in Nicaragua
> in Zimbabwe
> in strugglin' South Africa

The revolution reclaims many things even as it opens new horizons in education and morality. Above all it reclaims change as the eternal theme in nature and human society..

> de change
> an' de promise
> of de change
> is sweet and strong.

But change, movement, growth emerge from a contradiction. The dialectics of change are at the heart of the poem *Butterfly*.

> The caterpillar dead
> The butterfly
> born.

The poem *Butterfly Born* and others like *The Lesson* and *Callaloo* are a powerful celebration — with all the excitement and the joy that go with celebration! — of a new people and a new life.

The revolution then embodies the dreams and visions of an awakened people. Not surprisingly, the image of the dream is the most dominant in the entire collection. In this Merle Collins joins another Caribbean revolutionary poet, Martin Carter, who celebrates the grandeur of all the struggling of the earth who sleep not to dream, but dream to change the world.

It is her consciousness that change is inevitable, that movement is not always along a straight line, and her commitment to the collective dream of Grenadian masses for a world in which they own the earth and the sweat that works the earth, that makes Merle Collins,

the poet, not despair when the revolution suffers a
double blow: the disintegration of the leadership and
the invasion of Grenada by U.S. imperialist forces.

Of course the pain and the sorrow are there. The
pain hurts particularly when the poetess contemplates
the disintegration of the leadership. In the poem *To
Trample Dreams*, she says:

> If you had moved
> beyond the realm
> of unbelief
> if you had moved
> to trustin'
> if you had moved
> to stretchin' out your hand
> to touch the warmth
> of the spoken struggle
> for justice
> for food
> for education
> if you
> my friend
> had moved to believin'
> that the struggle
> was one struggle
>
> then your pain
> is my pain
> your unbelief
> is my distress
>
> you too
> watch now
> with wisdom
> born of living pain
> how we chose
> a golden platter
> to hand across our dreams

She comes back to the same point in the poem *Rock-
Stone Dance*:

And to think
that you
and I
let fall those dreams
and gave that gaping crowd
the chance to shout
for shells
to shower
shocking
blessings
on our soil!

But she also sings with pain to those who, imbued with a colonial mentality, welcomed the U.S. imperialist invasion of Grenada. In a poem called *A Song of Pain* she captures brilliantly the essence of neo-colonial mentality in those 'who have learnt so well the lesson of self-rejection'.

You use their words
to call
your sister
your brother
terrorist
learnt so well
the lesson of your conquerors
that now you, too
feel certain
you are too ignorant
to determine your destiny

so you welcome their invasions
echoing their words
you call their rape
deliverance . . .

The U.S. imperialist invasion of Grenada tries to trap the revolution. The invasion wants to crush all the dreams, all the visions, all the possibilities of building a new world as described in *Callaloo* and *Butterfly Born*. The poet who had been created by the revolution, and

who had been part of the revolutionary awakening of
Grenada, watches U.S. imperialism rolling in to ensure
that Grenada remains a neo-colonial backyard of Uncle
Sam. In the poem *Rock-Stone Dance* she says

> I watched
> like easter-morning
> through the egg-whites
> of our shattered dreams
> the ships that came
> to scorn my tears
> to mock our dreams
> to launch the planes
> to drop the bombs
> that ripped the walls
> that raped the land
> that burnt the earth
> that crushed the dreams
> that we all built.

But despite the pain, despite the sense of temporary
loss, despite the attempted murder of the revolution,
the poetess refuses to succumb to despair. In a poem
called *Fear* she rejects the neo-colonial culture of *Fear
and Silence* to proclaim:

> we were always afraid
> till we understood
> that our fear
> was their greatest weapon!

The revolution has taught her that nobody, no force on
earth, can turn back the clock of history. 'Water cannot
run uphill'.

In *Because the Dawn Breaks* she is all defiance,
proclaiming once again all the ideals of the revolution.
The dreams of the Grenadian masses will not be tram-
pled, and will never be finally crushed by U.S. steel.

> We speak
> because we dream

because
our dreams are not of living in pig pens
in any other body's
backyard
not of
catching crumbs from tables
not of crawling forever . . .

She is sure that Grenadian people will fight back, will
still affirm their history which has roots in Fedon, in
Toussaint, in Che, in Castro, in Cabral, in all the peasants
and workers of the earth.

We speak
for the same reason
that
the flowers bloom
that the sun sets
that the fruit ripens

U.S. led imperialism is only the dark hour before
revolutionary dawn. In the united struggles of workers
and peasants, in their total rejection of vassaldom,

hope screams forth
revolutions merge
to touch the pulse
of all that's beauty

We hope again
We live again
And dream again
to love forever.

Merle Collins speaks to more than Grenada. This collec-
tion of her poems belongs to Asia, to Africa, to Latin
America, to all those in the world who are struggling to
create a new world free from U.S. imperialism and all
the other forms of parasitism:

And I
> want to kick
> and scream
> and tear down
> and rebuild
>
> Then shall the wretched
> be the peacemakers
> to inherit all kingdoms
> All kingdoms
> present
> All kingdoms
> to come.

Yes, may it dawn!

Ngugi Wa Thiong'o
July, 1985

Publisher's Note

There is a struggle between two forms of poetry. One is concerned with assisting in the process of liberation and the other seeks to divert our attention from those issues which we must grapple with in order to clear the path towards our freedom. The poet in order to play a meaningful role in this process must, among other things, be an educator giving strength to the struggles we wage.

Karia Press, by publishing this collection , celebrates the tradition of committed writing. In the majority of cases works such as this has not been given access to the publishing medium and are left to lie and decay. But the ideas never die. They live on within the oral traditions of our societies. Our struggles, today, demand an approach which maximises the both the audience and the impact. It is in order to contribute towards this that Karia has published this powerful collection by Merle Collins. The act of publishing the work also reflects confidence that nothing can stop the march towards true independence.

The dawn will surely break!

Photographs & Illustrations

Acknowledgements

Most of this work is a result of the experiences of the Grenada Revolution and was written during 1978 to 1985. Read as a whole, the work represents specific moments, different responses, the pain and joy and beauty and doubt and hope of a total, still developing, defiantly positive experience.

Dedicated
to the Grenadian people

In appreciation
for the efforts
of the People's Revolutionary Government
which encouraged
our written expressions
and revived
our powerful oral traditions

In appreciation
to
the women of Old Westerhall
who gave shape
to my first oral presentations
within Grenada

In appreciation
to my mother
oral poetess and dramatist
whom old structures
buried within
house and home

In appreciation
to the members of African Dawn
whose work with the integration

of various art forms
has unravelled for me
new dimensions of creativity
and in particular
to
Kwesi Owusu
without whose critical assistance
many important technical aspects
would have gone unnoticed.

In appreciation
to all comrades
who have criticised
and argued
encouraged and supported
to give shape to this work

Merle Collins
July, 1985

Nabel–String

The part of me
That is there
not here
Home
not wandering
Not
chickee baby
Not
Hey sugar
how you doin' baby?
But
Doodoo darlin'
you awright?

Not
goin' up
to this enclosed home
in the elevator
on stairs
in silent
unconcerned
instinctive hostility
with the neighbour
I do not know
Not
turning the key
for the umpteenth time
in the door of 204
and suddenly
pausing
intent
attention on 203 ....

I wonder
who livin' dere?

No
not that
absence
of you
of me
of warmth
of life

But
running outside
wid de
piece o' bread
Ay!
Teacher Clearie!

Shout de bus for me
nuh
Ay! James! Wait!
Take de
kerosene pan.
Chupes!
Ah doh takin'
no damn
kerosene pan
Eh!
But he ignorant eh!
Bring it! Bring it!
Ca dammit!

There
Where neighbour
is friend
and enemy
to be cussed
and caressed
so damn annoyin'
you could scream
sometimes
so blasted fas'
in you business
you could hate

most times

But hate
is feeling
lovin'
an' cussin'
an' laughin'
an' needin'
is livin'

That blank stare
From the
unknown
next door
neighbour
kills something inside
makes the warmth inside
bring the tears

And the sound
of the heart
beat
of the drum
beat
is River Sallee[1]
is Arnold
feelin'
soarin'
is Frank
not understanding
is Victoria
is Belmont
is down in the Mang
by de cinema dey

You
I
We
left
left to search

1   River Sallee, Victoria, Belmont, the Mang: places in Grenada.

as always
for a better life
to escape the lime[1]
by de "quay-say" dey
by de lance dey
by Buy-Rite[2] dey
to find jobs
to chase
education

"Go on chile
take what ah din get
you hear
ah has no money to leave
all ah have
is in you head"

Left because
every year
more out o' school
less work to get
becus de landless wid money
get land
an de widdout money landless
was still more landless yet[3]
and still lovin'
because of a memory

Because Chemistry
in form Five
dis year
An' limin'
on Market Hill[4]

1. Liming: Standing about talking or observing events.
2. Quay-Say, Lance, Buy-Rite: Local liming spots.
3. Reference to land re-distribution scheme called "land for the landless",
4. Reference to a land re-distribution scheme called "land for the landless",
   started by Eric Gairy in the latter half of the nineteen seventies, before
   his overthrow by the New Jewel Movement.
   Market Hill: steep incline in the middle of the city of St. George's,
   Grenada.

straight
for de whole
o' nex' year
jus'
din kin' o' make
no sense

Because love turned hate
is bitter not sweet
an' when you cousin
de secret police
beat you up
an' search you
an' treaten
to report you
you feel
like you dyin'
inside
an' bein' reborn
of hate
and that
hurts

Left too
Because of
a need
to search
for the reason
the beginning
the end
the all
so left
and will always
be leaving

But the pull
of the heart
beat
of the drum
beat

Ay!
Bury de chile
nabel-string[1]
under de
coconut-tree
you know
By way
I did bury
she fadder own
So de nabel-string dey
An' as de palm
branch
swayin'
it pullin'
it pullin'

Ay - y !!

---

1.   Umbilical cord.

My Space

Hovering on the brink
Of eternity
Searching the existing
To find the true
Questioning the shallow depth
Of man's intimate relations
Humbly arrogant
Painfully humble
Beauty the truth
not yet discovered
And this vast ugliness
Painfully lonely
Here
Hovering on the brink
Of tremblingly full eternity

The Search

I remember

The form
of my guilt
The blackness
of the dotted line
on the white paper
Name
Okay
Nationality?
Pen poised
Hand encircling paper now
Guilty fingers seeking
To hide
Nationality?

Friend
Absorbed too
Looked up
Well, Name
filled in
Nationality
Trinidadian
Held my breath
Hoping not to be reminded
That I
Complete with Irish name
Like hers
Was not yet Grenadian
But still ... British
Jesus Christ!
British!

But
Her own pen poised

She
Struggled with her own
Mammoth problem
Race?
Looked at my hand
Below
At the neatly pencilled
"African"
Goggled
Grinned
Said with awe
I put
"Black"

Shrugged
Looked at each other
Caught in the strange dilemma
Of non-belonging
Down again at the paper
Aspiring social-scientists
Sought
Next dotted line
On the tutor's paper
Social strata?
You put
Lower class?
Giggle
Giggle

Okay
I mean
What else?
What else?
Sitting on the balcony
of Block B
Within the far from
Lower class
Walls of Mona[1]
Two of the region's

---

1   Jamaica campus of the University of the West Indies.

Privileged few
Ashamed to be
Anything but
What they called
In their forms
Lower class

Unsure of the claim
Unsure of much
Sure of wrong
Sure of search
Unwitting revolutionaries
Feeling the birth pains
Of moulding
A future belonging

I remember
the form of the past
foretelling
the shape
of things to come

The Beat Goes On

The beat goes on
And the planet's people die
Steeped in shit
Or slink off
with a look of
Guilt
and fear
Guilty of sins
unasked for
unnamed
non-existent
The meek
waiting to inherit
The earth
And they must
feel the taste of
Failure
Bitter
in the mouth

Didn't want
to be born
to perch
huddled together
over the river
in huts
waiting to fall
begging to be seen
by those big houses
on the other side
All children
of that same
Distant God
some more equal
than others

Every time
the big man
shakes his head
and says
These people
Man
They have no ambition
The scream
inside my head
brings the tears

And I
want to kick
and scream
and tear down
and rebuild

You
sit there
sure in the knowledge
of your own
present salvation
and know
that the eye
of the needle
will expand
that the camel
will enter
to secure his heaven

And
the wretched scream
Tired of waiting
at your urging
To inherit
a non-existent
Earth
And the scream
will expand
like the eye
of your

imaginary needle
Reshape
and create
Eternal beauty

Then shall the wretched
be the peacemakers
to inherit all kingdoms
All Kingdoms
Present
All Kingdoms
To come

The Lesson

You tink
was a easy lesson?
Was a
deep lesson
A well-taught
lesson
A
carefully-learnt
lesson

I
could remember
Great Grand-Mammy
Brain tired
And wandering
Walkin' an' talkin'
Mind emptied and filled
Bright
Retaining
And skilfully twisted
By a sin
Unequalled by Eve's
Great Grand-Mammy
Living proof
Of de power
of de word
Talked knowingly
Of William de conqueror
Who was de fourth son
Of de Duke of Normandy
He married Matilda
His children were
Robert
Richard
Henry
William and

Adella

Grannie
Mind going back
Teachin' what she knew
Pick on de boss frien'
on de boss hero
William de conqueror
My frien'
Is your frien'
But your frien'
Not my frien'

Grannie
Din remember
No Carib[1] Chief
No Asante king
For Grannie
Fedon never existed
Toussaint[2]
Was a
Whispered curse
Her heroes
Were in Europe
Not
In the Caribbean
Not
In Africa
None
In Grenada

Her geography
Was
Of de Arctic Ocean
An' de Mediterranean

1 The Callinagos, the indigenous peoples virtually exterminated by
   the Europeans when they took the Caribbean countries. Carib,
   first used as a derogatory term for the Callinagos, is the name by
   which the indigenous people are now generally known.
2 Toussaint L'Ouverture, black Haitian revolutionary leader, of late
   18th century.

She spoke of
Novasembla
Francis-Joseph Land
And Spitbergin
In de Arctic Ocean
Of Ireland
And de
pharoah islands
belong to Denmark
Spoke
Parrot-like
Of
Corsica
Sardinia
Sicily
Malta
de Lomen islands
An' de islands
Of de Archipelago
In de
Mediterranean

Is not
No Nancy-Story
Nuh
Is a serious
joke
I use to
laugh at Grannie
Repeat after her
Till one day
Ah check de map
Fin' de spellin'
little different
To how
I did think
But de geography
Straight
Like a arrow
Tip focusing
On de

Arctic ocean

Den
Me blood
run cole
Me eyes
stay fix
on de Arctic Circle
Watchin'
Spitsbergen
And Franz Josef Land
Watchin'
Lower down
De Faer Oer Islands
In Denmark Strait
Unaccountably feeling
the cold grip of the Arctic
Noting how
by a cruel trick
Grannie's mind
Knew more of this
Than of a Grenada
Of a Caribbean
Which did not exist

A wandering star
Spun out of orbit
When the world
For an eternal moment
Went
A little too fast

Teach the slaves
And their children
And their children's
children
To know and live for
Our world
No new creation
Just a part

Of the great everlasting
Old
Arctic
And Mediterranean

And now
We
Consciously
Anti-colonial
Understanding all dat
And a little more
Will cherish
Grannie's memory
And beckon William across
To meet and revere
Our martyrs
Fedon[1]
And Toussaint
And Marryshow[2]
And Tubal Uriah Buzz
Butler[3]
And the countries
And principles
They fought for
We
Will watch
William's astonished admiration
As he humbly meets
Fidel[4]
As
In a spirit's daze
He greets the PRG[5]
We will move
Even closer

1 Julien Fedon, leader of 1795 Grenada uprising against the British.
2 Theophilus Albert Marryshow, Grenadian journalist, trade
   unionist and politician, known as the 'father' of the idea of
   Caribbean federation.
3 Grenadian who was at the forefront of the political, social and
   economic struggles in the Trinidad oilfields in the 1930s.
4 Cuban president Fidel Castro.
5 People's Revolutionary Government of Grenada, 1979–1983.

To watch Morgan de Pirate
Hide his loot
As we start
On our budget

In this beginning
We
Will rewrite
De history books
Put William
On de back page
Make Morgan
A
footnote

Grannies to come
Will know
Of de Arctic Ocean
But will know more
Of the Caribbean Sea
Of the Atlantic Ocean

We
Will recall with pride
Our own
So
Goodbye William
Good
Riddance
Welcome
Fedon
Kay sala sé sa'w[1]
Esta es
su casa
This is
your home!

1. Patwa: Translated in the final two lines. Patwa is a language spoken by
   some of the older people in Grenada and more widely spoken in St. Lucia,
   Dominica, Martinique and Guadeloupe. It is a result of African rhythms
   and speech structures combined with the French colonial experience.

Callaloo

Mix up
like callaloo[1]
Not no watery callaloo
But
a thick, hot, sweet
callaloo
burnin' you tongue
Wid dem chunk o' dumplin'
goin' down nice
an' wid coconut
wid o' widdout deaders
as de case may be
as de taste may be
as de pocket may be
but sweet
an' hot

Dat is what it feel like
to be part o' dis
Revolution reality
O' dis
wakin' up reality
o' dis
no more hidin' you passport
reality
no more
hangin' you head
an' shufflin' you foot
an' tryin' to hide
behin' de person
in front o' you
like little Janet
behin' she mudder skirt

1 Popular soup made from the leaf of the dasheen plant.

when de man ask
"whey you from?"

No more
playin' you doh hear
or sayin' some shit like
A...a..a...island
near by Trinidad
Or
a...a few mile
off Venezuela
but out loud an' bole
like you make de name
GRENADA!

An' wid you head in de air
becus de world is yours
an' you know is yours
an' you not goin' be
meek
meek
meek
an' wait to see
if
somebody
goin' let you
inherit the earth
becus you know arready
is yours

so you say
loud
an' clear
an' proud
GRENADA!

an' you silent scream
which he musbe hear
becus he look up
into your claimin' eyes
says
Dat mean Revolution

Dat mean Progress
Dat mean Forward!
Dat mean
sharin'
an' carin'
an' believin'
an' livin'
an' lovin'

Dat mean
a country in the Caribbean
in Latin America
in the Americas
in the struggle
in the world

Dat mean, Comrade
a people
like de people
in Cuba
in Nicaragua
In Zimbabwe
in Mozambique
in strugglin' South Africa
in all dem countries
whey de people know
dat doh donkey say
de worl' ain't level
even donkey heself
musbe does shake he head
to feel dem bumps
an' know

how t'ing so hard
for some toe
an' so sof'
for others

All o' we
in all o' dis worl'
so mix up

like callaloo
an' yet
so not like callaloo
an' dat is why
de change
an' de promise
of de change
is sweet an' strong

like de soup
w'en Grannie
cover it down dey
an' let it
consomme
like dat
hot
sweet
burnin'
heavy
heavy

ca - lla - loo !

The Butterfly Born

Something old
Something new
Something borrowed
Something blue

The caterpillar dead
The butterfly
born

Alé asiz anba tab-la!
Zòt fouten twop.[1]
Go an' siddown under de table!
You too fas'.
You tink it easy?
Even wid all o' dat
Wid de mudder shoutin'
In days long ago
Dat little girl
Used to walk two, three days a week
From St David's town
By the police station
Where she Mammie use to work
Right up to Sauteurs town
By de ball-pitch groun'
Afraid of she shadow
of de basket shadow
of she dress shadow
of de fig-leaf shadow
But walkin' alone
all kin' o' hour
Hidin' an' cryin' an' hatin'
Becus she Mammie
couldn't afford it

1 Patwa. Translated in the two lines immediately following.

An' to besides
Was really a waste
o' good money
To pay de bus a whole
eight pence ha'penny

De biggest girl of five
Walkin' to bring
de little piece o' bread
de two grain o' bluggoe
for Iona an' Joycelyn an' Jude
an' Stephen
To keep body an' soul togedder
Woman-chile
A giant of nine
Strong since den
Strong even when bathed
in tears
Strong when blisters formed
from walking
A strong
premature
nine-year-old mother

Part of the history
Part of de life
De strength inherited
De weakness taught
Something old
Something true

I
must remember dat day
when Auntie Iona come from
England
I
Hold on to de blin'
An' watch Mammie
in de sittin' room
An Auntie Iona
nice nice nice
Wid earring
an' stocking

an' lipstick
an' ting

Auntie
Auntie
Iona
Oh hello!
Isn't that
Antoinette?

An' Mammie
So vex she could bus'
She face
tellin' de story
Of dogs among doctors
Of little girl who
don' know dey place
An' I
squeezin' back
behin'
de blin'
Not darin' to answer
One Ionic question
Lookin' straight
At Mammie face
An' slinkin' back

Behin'
de blin'

Den come
de eruption
De whispered
benediction
Clear out
Kadammit fout[1]
Children
must know dey place

---

1 Possibly a mixture of progressive Patwa 'ka', English 'dammit' and Patwa
   'fout' meaning 'damn'.

An' especially
little girl
Somebody
talkin' to you?
Outside!
All you always dey
To make people shame

Something borrowed
Something
blue

Mother
Teaching
As she was taught
Little girls
Must learn
To be seen not heard
Or is certain
destruction
Is pillar of saltness
Oh God!
Look how Lot
smart
An' he wife
so fas'
A pillar of salt!

De lesson
passed on
Alé asiz anba tab-la!
Zòt fouten twop
Dammit fout
Chile
Nuttin' good
Could come out o' you
Little girl like you
Only rompin' an' runnin'
An' climbin' tree
Like dose little boy
Oh Jesus

De Lord
Give me a trial
An' is me
people go blame
Yuh know

Woman-chile
Crying for the world
Crying for me
Crying because
I couldn't find their Eve
Who
In times past
Had shouted
When told to whisper
And lived
To expose
De deadly truth
Dat de wages of sin
Is life
before death

Sa ki fè'w?
Sa ou ka pléwe pou?
What wrong wid you?
What you cryin' for?
Vini tifi[1]
vini
vini
mwen kay héle ba'w
I go bawl for you

Something
blue

Wid a lesson
like dat
1979[2]

1 Patwa: Come, little girl.
2 The New Jewel Movement came to power in Grenada on
   March 13th 1979.

not no easy ting
But de strength was dey
De weakness imposed
De adventure was dey
De spirit just hushed
Now
woman-chile
woman
All of a sudden
Not under no table
But out in de open

Demanding equal
recognition
For equal beauty given

Something new
Something true

From
Zòt fouten twòp
You too fas'
To Woman step forward
To Woman
Equal in Defense
Huh
You tink it easy?

Something new
Something true

What that mean?
You tink is a puzzle?
Something dead
Something born

But
De caterpillar's death
De butterfly's birth
Is only a miracle
If you doh know

de story
Is only a mystery
if you doh know the history
Is only truly
a puzzle
If you can't find
the pieces
If you can't explain
de changes

Is de beauty of science
If you follow
the history
Is the poetry of science
If you watch
de movement
Famn
Alé douvan
Woman
Step forward
Something new
Something true

The caterpillar dead
The butterfly born!

Magnetic

The distance
The sea
The town
My world
This land is mine
And I
have the title paper
to every grain
of sand

I listen
do not respond
But know
it is
the land I own
The plane zooms in
My ears are stopped
The noise so loud
I feel the noisy silence
Touch down
and I
am big with joy
and pride
and small
and sad
And so filled
with love
that I feel foolish
and strong with pride

Home again
My land

Home once again
The magnet land

Is this it?
There again the voice
That other voice
Yep!
This it!
Grenada eh?
Well
let's see
I look at him
Whisper loudly
inside my head
See nothing
Mr Tour-er!
This is it!
I dare you to ...
Nothing
Just dare you ...
Not to love
But then
it doesn't matter
as you please

I try to keep from smiling
Try to keep from bursting
Home again
See all faces
See no faces
Sea of faces
Home again

Or in by boat
And watch that beauty
Watch those birds
Watch that land
Watch that sea
Watch them
All together
And learn the language
That will never
be written
Not ever be spoken

Watch that lovely land

Don't need no smoke
Get high on eye-
power
Just watch
that green
and brown
and black
and white
and love-
ly land

Revelation

So he's an artist
Poor fool
A poet
No less

One of those beings
Whose hearts may shout
But hands don't go up
In vulgar display
Of emotions felt
Often unfelt
Not analysed to the full

No rushing cry of forward
No stinging revolutionary shout
Though the thought may be there
The feeling even deeper
Than many a shouted support

May be happy with the dog
Not with its bite
So will nod at the lick
And wince at the bite
Won't lick no asses
To summon the praise

He's a poet
Poor fool
I know of the type
A poet
No less

The Feather

A lifting breeze
A quick movement
A child's anguished scream
A mother's anxious question
No pain
Only fear
Dissipated by touch
And proof
Just a feather
With no life of its own
Moved by the breeze
Not attacking you
Just moving
Because of the breeze
See? A feather
Hold it
Go on
Hold it
Feather?
Yes
Just a feather

But we
were orphans
So our feathers
Had horns
Each breeze
Was a hurricane
1959
Was a storm
Anguished scream
Firm explanation
Yes
Fear now
Pain later

Except perhaps you pray
to dissipate the evil
That Castro could bring

Castro?
Sh-h-h!
Not so loud
Don't ask questions
Don't seek to know
Just pray
That such evil be contained

A lifting breeze
A quick movement
Cuba moved on
The Caribbean looked inward
Embraced
By discerning
Europe
But some of the imprisoned
Lifted their eyes
Sought their own answers
Next time
No scream
Felt the breeze
Saw the feather
Picked it up
Touched
Questioned each other
Lamented the deception
That so long
Excluded a comrade

Beyond

Beyond
Way over dey
But near here
And far in de distance
Because dis ting
Dis Revolution
Dis change
Dis growin'
Not easy to explain
So much a part
Of you and me
That we
Could talk about it
And explain
Why the progress
Is ours
The growth
Is ours
The movement
Is ours
But so big an' great
Dat it leave you cold
An' hot
An' proud
An' glad
An' kin' o' dam frighten
An' wonderin'
But strong
An' kin' o' humble an'
fierce
An' ready to fight
An' so much kin' o'
mix-up ting
Dat after a time
You jus' stop
Try to explain

An' live the silence
Of shoutin'
Wid all de comrades
Not jus' here
But there an' here
Way over dey
Zimbabwe
Nicaragua
Cuba
Mozambique
Angola
Way out yonder
Into the vast
Shouting silence
Of beyond

Tears

I cry for the world
I cry for me
I cry because
the deep end
feels so close
And I want
to walk
over and out
into unremembering nothing
I have failed
to grasp
to put meaning
to understand
to love this
And I want to
walk
to run
to go

Just Suddenly So

All of a sudden
It not nice again
Jus' suddenly so
Wid a funny kind o'
Reasonless reason
De experience turn sour
Is not a adventure again
Mouse-trap smiles clang suddenly shut

The power wand waves sometimes
With a gentleness
Suspect because employed
And withdrawn at will
Smiles come and go
Kicks, kisses
Come, go
Fly, Live, Die

And I
Bewildered
Silently vow
To keep screaming
Low and loud
Not to be caught
By gentleness idly tossed
Idly withdrawn

To move
To grow
To live, to grow
To cry, to grow
To die and not to wilt
To shout
And insist on growing

Be Free

My dream of ships
of people
of waiting decks
and eager lines
Moving quickly towards
Distress
You say
Too soon awake perhaps
but better the unfinished dream
than distressing news
Better to destroy the image
fashioned by a mind
eager to drink
the heady draught of shared creation
Awed by the lilting tilt
of the free bird's wing
the sibilant flow
of beauty on the wing
But unable to release
My particular bird
to wing its way

Away

To sunlit creation
Grasping with greedy fingers
the beauty I love to watch
Fascinated
Released and flowing
Beauty real if impersonal
Loving perhaps freedom and beauty
in abstract
Yet seeking to capture the essence
Watching the caged bird
expecting to enjoy the beauty

of the bird on the wing
But the caged bird wilts

Losing the sibilance
Through unreasoning fear
Destroying the beauty I seek to
hold
So I release
and watch you soar
enjoy again the beauty
Try not to mind
that your life is yours
Watch you fall
and hurt
and mend your wing
and dance
and falter
and dip and soar
and curtsy your own love of life
and love in answer to my prayer
Winging away into the beautiful
Blinding sunlight
To make true my dream of ships
Which did not sail
So no distress
Just unharnessed beauty on the
Wing

Dreams

Will not cling to dreams
Will not
strive to bottle
rainbow beauty
Will take the moment's
Magic
Love the essence
Tremble with the longing
Hold close the clinging pain
Of caring
for all essence
But cannot cling to dreams
Will
Perhaps
In spite of all
My friends non-believing
Spite of all
Society's urging
Spite of all
those centuries teaching
Will perhaps
remain suspended
wondering sure
living love
And cling to dreams
Dreaming alive
Living dreams
Alone
In a crowd of non-believers
Who will be converted

The Embrace

When I hold you close
for an eternal moment
and touch with my face
one cheek
the other

lingering heartbeats
speak worlds of love
of hope
for teeming millions

as we embrace
Revolutions touch
building beauty
that people let slip

hope
screams forth
Revolutions merge
to touch the pulse
of all that's beauty

We hope again
We live again
And dream again
to love forever

Sh – h – h–!

Be quiet
Words born of pain
And oozing with hurt
Are often not worth
The paper they're on

Glimpses

lost the way
wandering star
spinning without motion
speeding
no direction
living the journey
an indecisive haven
dreading arrival
purposefully
spinning
pointlessly
glimpses of heaven
in deafening chaos
the end the beginning
the stillness of motion
intellectual laziness
elusive substance
quiet ignorance
in humble arrogance
lost the way

don't seek no linkages
hopscotch the essence

a moment's madness?
or
the truth of craziness?

Free

Born free
to be caught
and fashioned
and shaped
and freed to wander
within
a caged dream
of tears

From Up Above

Green
slight bumps
on the open palm
Houses
red
white
and rooftop dots

A boat
an island
hugged
by a jealously green
warmly blue
and loving arm
of sea

One of the islands
I
Caribbean woman
am proud to own

A rainbow
fleeting
streaks approval
through the fluffy clouds
and cloudy wisps
pause to chat
and tell the tale
of islands
green
brown
and warmly
blue

As I
yearn

to capture
the essence
uncapturable
majestic
white cloud mountains
standing firmly
in the open blue

telling the tale
of space
and chaos
warning
of the vastness
of narrow space
the empty fulness
of a
poignant
pregnant
sky
holding in thrall
the mind
of the
poet scientist
speaking of future
and past
and eternity
and pain
and beauty

Fluffy non-existence
hiding the beautiful
painful truth
of sea
and land
and life below
stern white gendarmes
in the calculating blue
waiting to spin
and
drunkenly somersault
if the

metal giant's
heartbeat
ceased to pulse

On through
mocking blue
emptiness
then
the giant
cocky bird
dips
one cocksure wing
kicks out
defiant wheels
to shoot
a fiery
farewell kick
at mocking space

zooms in
hovers
concentrates
swoops in again
on distant buildings

cold
awe - ful
awesome
calculatingly
impressive

hovers
five extra minutes
caught
in the rush
of other birds
to that
frightening city
prayerfully hovers
lowers

walks wearily

the length
of the island
left behind
journey over
Journey begun

The Loudest Song

Beautiful night
splash of light
fervent voices
raised in song
In Nicaragua
Fernando Gordillo[1]
tells
how struggle
is
the loudest song

The beat goes on
the worms roll out
the rats will gnaw
the prowling cat
goin' tief a chance
to jump up high
an' grab the cream

But
Si Nicaragua venció
El Salvador vencerá
y Guatemala seguirá
If Nicaragua won
El Salvador
will win
and Guatemala
will follow

Comandante Ana Maria
Dead
for boundless love

---

1   The poem was written after a 1983 Festival of Song in Nicaragua which
     used as its theme the words of Latin American Artiste Fernando Gordillo
     "Struggle is the loudest song".

for deeper faith
for greater hope
shaken faith
vengeful storm
maddening pain
A thousand questions
A hundred answers

the heart will scream
the children weep
the country bleeds

the struggle never stops
Revolutions
never die

Si Nicaragua venció
El Salvador vencerá
y Guatemala seguirá

In Asia
Africa
Latin America
The Caribbean
Venceremos
We will win

We scream
to the spirits
dead and alive
to Che Guevara's eyes
that pierce the dreams
of constant time
that

Venceremos
We will win

From Courage
born of hurt
from Courage

born of pain
from Courage
born of
what we see
and what we know

and what we feel
and what will be
because it must
Venceremos

Nicaragua's pain
Palestine's hurt
strugglers' claim
what is to is
must is
a constant song
in praise of love
with Fernando Gordillo
we say

la lucha
es la más alta
de las canciones

Struggle is
the loudest song

Movements

1920
not one hundred years away
from the last ship
Out of Africa
Black woman
Black man
Needing still to shout
That
O mother Africa
I am yours
I am mine
And I
am not the filth
They say I am

Marcus Garvey
vision of progress
in unity
never been to Africa
but lived the fulfilling dream
of being a part
of some thing
that cared
more than he had ever known
and so
Africa
The home he never knew

Oh Africa
he cried
I'm hurt
Screaming then
with countless millions
for love and caring
oh Africa
I want my mama

an answer
like the red black and green
walking to prison shouting

I shall live

"look for me in the whirlwind
seek me in the storm
look for me all around you
I shall bring with me
countless millions
of black slaves
who have died"[1]
and we shall live again
For liberty
For freedom
For life again

Dream scarcely understood
unfolding
with tender loving strength
in different ways
in different tones
in different times

Marcus Garvey
taught to believe
that black was dark
and white light
was always right
screamed that
No
Africa and its children
will be free

To no longer see
The African
The Indian
of our America
depressed an' poor

1 Words of Marcus Garvey.

an' hungry
an' bawlin'
for a dead distant
stolen
motherland

To no longer see
The people of our Africa
of our America
holin' dey belly
an' bawlin'
for dey mudderlan'
for dey fadderlan'
for dey own lan'
to no longer see
we people
fail to see
de writin'
dat been standin' clear
right dey upon de wall
for countless generations

To no longer see
Caribbean sportsmen
Africa's sons
pocket the imperial cash
born of black sweat
and burning tears
grin white teeth
in sickening need
to justify the title
honorary white

once again so far
an' yet so near

And the world
weeps with Africa
and Africa understands with pain

dat traitors come
sometimes
in black white green yellow
an'
polka-dot

Dat all
who weep
for their land
mus' understand
why you weepin'
for your lan'

And Oh
Mother Africa
Oh Mother World
Garvey's dream moves on

And I
black woman
black human
dreaming dreams too
of freedom
Celau c'est celau
what is yours is yours
and Africa will be free

Garvey told then
how
now we have started to speak
he is only the forerunner
of an awakened Africa
that will never
go back to sleep

did not need to add
that being awake
you will speak

with ever-widening vision
the dream moves on

much learnt
much to learn
and so
soft or loud
Forward Ever
Never again asleep!

The Essence

The dreams
the hopes
the speaking vision
reaching out
to twist the arrant nonsense
out of non-essence
and scoff at petty pride
and narrow hurt
and touch the belly-button
heart
of distant
ever present time
holding all
spreadeagled like spiders
across the giant web
of people love
and people hurt
people taught
not to know
or trust
a national style

Politics?
Politricks!
politician and preacher
girl?
watch dem ps!

an' furthermore
don't trust no man
girl
dem jus' born
to give woman
splittin' head
ache

taught never to trust
taught words born big
in another person's mind-
less-ness
all you know
and all you need to know
like bad system
an' good system
communism versus capitalism
like bad black
an' good white
How de hell you mean why?
I say so
is why

But some whys
screamed out
with all our hurt
that some still choose
to skin teet
an' bow head
yes Massa suh
I asks no question suh
Is so suh

But still
the vision lives
is crushed
caught
dies
to live again
as thousands more
are born
and questions grow
and many more of us
are caught
spreadeagled
in a web of love
and trust
moulding the truth
that must exist
in ever-present time

Trapped

Butterfly
trapped in a mould
of molten steel
wings open
poised for flight
caught by more
than the matter seen
wish I knew where history been
wish I knew
where they make the fire
that melt the steel
that make the prison
to hold the butterfly
that spirits made

Poems Moved

A poem moved that day
eyes pierced the distance
touching with the heart
the scattered stars
pulling together myriad stars
as Maurice talked
of Caricom
and neighbour's tricks
the pelting kicks
that never hit
of how history tried
to live again
mistakes long gone
and cut the ties of Caricom[1]

Maurice talked[2]
and Che's eyes flashed
and touched the essence
of living love
as Maurice talked
of Caricom
and people's hopes
and people's lives
and living dreams
Caricom will live
and we will live
Caricom will grow
as Grenada grows
Caricom will move
and reach new heights
and touch the truth

1 The Caribbean Community, a grouping established in 1973.
2 The poem is the result of Maurice Bishop's address to the
   Grenadian people after the Caricom Heads of Government
   Meeting held in Trinidad and Tobago, 4 July 1983.

and scorn the waste
of passing kicks
and dirty tricks

So a poem moved
as Maurice talked
and the people watched
and the silence screamed
with living love
Five on canvas[1]
sharing the beauty
of people love

Fidel upright
eyes steady and clear
sighting the tricks
of busy kicks
Michael swearing
never again
to move his eyes
and let target slip
with people's bliss
and Che alone
looking way out yonder
commanding space
to give its essence
to create the truth
and leave the waste
of careless kicks
Che's eyes pierced
and Maurice talked
and a poem moved that day

The faces watched
the faces loved
the faces talked
the faces loved
Maurice talked
and Maurice loved
and poems moved that day

1   In the room were paintings of Michael Manley, Fidel Castro,
    Che Guevara, Daniel Ortega and Maurice Bishop.

For Che

He has
eager eyes
that move
beyond the letter
to the spirit
beyond
the negativity
of despair

to hope
to dream

to expose the lie
that dreams die
to glorify the truth
that dreamers wake
to live visions

speaking eyes
that make you think
namelessness
and spirit
and soul
and beauty
and essence

eyes that hold
all the promise
of the past
all the glory
of the future
all the eagerness
of the
poet-dreamer

fighter
lover
revolutionary

whose cry
will not be stilled
who scorns
the narrow confines
of limiting identity

to span
the limitless
space
across the nations
and live
and live
forever

for spirits
never die

Fear

Afraid
born afraid
turned around
and shuddered with fear
till forced by the knife
to look at the light
to scream with the fear
of ghosts unknown

afraid
always afraid

still at the corner
of a clamouring world
assuming a calm
in the teeth
of the storm

afraid
of the love
that binds
and demands
fearing the bond
that assumes
and controls

afraid to disappoint
faith
hope
the pain of life
in the teeth of the storm
the fear of the strife
to which we were born

afraid
always afraid

timidity fed
by blessings for the meek
fearing the power
that binds
and creates

afraid
we were always afraid
until we understood
that our fear
was
their greatest weapon.

Behind Shutters

I knew
I had heard it
somewhere before

he said
his father lived
behind shutters
like
"if once
you let yourself care
the crying
might never stop"

and listening
to the printed word
I looked back
over the years
at a face
absorbing the shock
of the idea
of not liking
to be liked

and knew again
the continuing truth
that
whether you admit or not
to caring
once you let yourself
care
for the abstract
or the live

the crying
might never stop

but then again
the joy
might never end

To Trample Dreams

If you had moved
beyond the realm
of unbelief
if you had moved
to trustin'
if you had moved
to stretchin' out your hand
to touch the warmth
of the spoken struggle
for justice
for food
for education
if you
my friend
had moved to believin'
that the struggle
was one struggle

then your pain
is my pain
your unbelief
is my distress

you too
watch now
with wisdom
born of living pain
how we chose
a golden platter
to hand across our dreams

standing ant-like now
in a spinning
roaring chaos
become

so many Judases
so many Simon-Peters
I tell you again
I know not him

But ask
dat man dere
dis woman here
Dat
is one o' dem

... a ten dollars please
people must live

An' dat
is one o' dose
who dared to hope
dat better must come

Now we
clutching close
thirty pieces of shining silver
reflecting
in our hopes
brand new
houses of pleasure
dollars of leisure
survival of the fittest
new times
new rhymes
play de tunes dem
let me dance
a lively death-mask jig
like a tender puppet
on a livin' string

It hurts when you say
that
people must learn to skip
people must learn
to sleep
people must live

people running
screaming
stepping movie steps
over 50 foot walls
to trample dreams
and remember
Maurice
Saying
June 19, 1980

"When we consider the list
of those who have died
those who may yet die
and those who are injured ...
you can get an idea
of the point I am making"

And now we
can only say
what a way
to make a point!
"They can kill our bodies"
he said
"they can never kill the spirit"

And even though
the they
is now
a literary exercise

perhaps
just perhaps
when Balthazar river
come down
an' de bridge overflow

we mus' know den
to pass roun' de road

1. Reference to speech by Maurice Bishop in June, 1980, after a bomb
   planted at Queen's Park, St. George's killed and injured several people.
2. River with a low bridge, in the north-east of Grenada.

so much lost
so much to lose

perhaps
just perhaps
the darkest hour
is right before the dawn

The Signs

and the dogs knew
countless weeks before
the dogs
raise dey head
an' howl
despair
an' shame
an' cry mourning
to the
quietly listening
stilly smiling
sky

the dogs knew

and I too
could remember
the story
me frien' did tell
of a spirit
wandering
restless
cut down
from the home
it loved
from the home
it knew
not knowin' where
to go
or where
to stay

and even when
I awoke
afraid
from my dream

of ships
of waiting decks
and eager
distressful
lines

I
could not believe

snake
could mean enemy
an' ship in dream
could mean
distress

But
for de sake o' de struggle
not such distress
for de sake o' de progress
for de sake
o' de change
for de sake
o' de promise
for de sake
o' de sense
for de sake
of the future essence

not such
a cutting down
to sink
in the painful shame
o' we blood
bathing

for de sake
o' de understandin'
listen to the school-
children
talk
'common' sense

and
for de sake
o' de calaloo

simmer down

Hurricane Janet[1] time
1955
was to see
de coconut-tree
dat yesterday
been standin'
in front o' de house
now lookin' like it plant
behin' de house

widdout branches
widdout head
widdout movement
all de cocoa tree dead
all de banana fall

den de calm
come
after de storm

plenty rip off
plenty tip off
but den
not all skin teet
is good grin
not all wag tail
is promise
not to bite

---

1. In 1955, a hurricane, Hurricane Janet, devastated the island..

Rock-Stone Dance

Handed you my dreams
like treasured eggs
held your eyes
touched your hands
for eternity's instant
in harmony with all
searching creation
for the elusive answer
uniquely
internationally
ours

Felt sure your dream
was mine
was theirs
was ours
was the latent dream
of all the world's poor

Together
we were
humbly
arrogantly
painfully
hopefully
sure

Then
your attention wavered
you turned to frown
to dispute the truth
we all shared
with another
who surely
must also

have
shared the dream

You
let slip my dream
and yours
and theirs
and ours
and as we all died
our different
distinct
similar
collective deaths

Painful
Grotesque
Shameful
Sad

I watched
like easter-morning
through the egg-whites
of our scattered dreams
the ships that came
to scorn my tears
to mock our dreams
to launch the planes
that dropped the bombs
that ripped the walls
that raped the land
that burnt the earth
that crushed the dreams
that we all built

and the marines
with Charity's righteous hand
the marines
who
charitably secure
love to bomb murderers
in distant lands

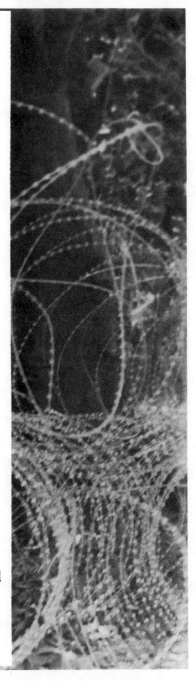

marines
both
white
and
black

who never thought
to bomb
the murderous
Klu-Klux Klan
From out of
their own land
never thought
to ruthlessly seek
those who murder
sons like

Malcolm X
and Martin Luther King

The kind marines
may stay
some sixty days
or more
perhaps
to be sure
that the natives
keep on grinning
simple-like

that America
keeps on winning
master-like

And to think
that you
and I
let fall those dreams
and gave that gaping crowd
the chance to shout
for shells

to shower
shocking
blessings
on our soil

God bless all
those sufferers
outside of
the U.S. of A.

And we
painfully learning
the lesson
so many spoke before

It ain't make no sense bawlin'
It ain't make no sense sittin' down
an' cryin'
Shake yourself
Go back outside

Egg have no right
in rock-stone dance

Because The Dawn Breaks

We speak
because
when the rain falls
in the mountains
the river slowly swells

Comes rushing down
over boulders
across roads
crumbling bridges
that would hold their power
against its force

We speak
for the same reason
that
the thunder frightens the child
that
the lightning startles the tree

We do not speak
to defy your tenets
though we do
or upset your plans
even though we do
or to tumble
your towers of babel
we speak
in spite of the fact
that we do

We speak
because
your plan
is not our plan

our plan
we speak because we dream
because
our dreams
are not of living in pig pens
in any other body's
backyard
not of
catching crumbs from tables
not of crawling forever
along the everlasting ant-line
to veer away in quick detour
when the elephant's foot
crashes down
not of having to turn back
when the smell of death
assails our senses
not of striving forever
to catch the image of your Gods
within our creation

We speak
for the same reason
that
the flowers bloom
that the sun sets
that the fruit ripens

because temples built
to honour myths
must crumble
as the dawn breaks
there is nothing you can do
about your feeble bridges
when the rain falls
in the mountains
and swells the flow of rivers

We speak
not to agitate you
but in spite of your agitation

because
we are workers
peasants
leaders
you see
and were not born
to be your vassals

A Song of Pain

I cannot sing to the wind
I cannot sing to space
I cannot sing only
to let others know
why the bush voices
speak so loudly in our land
and why sometimes
human hurricanes devastate

I cannot sing
only
to those who already know
that
over three hundred years and more
clever words
have been used as guns
and dragnets
for the conquest of our minds

I cannot feel content
to sing a quiet song
for I must sing too
with pain
to you, my sister
to you, my brother
who have learnt so well
the lesson of self-rejection
from your arrogant teacher's lips
that you cherish your meekness
to inherit their earth
leave to others your talent here
and seek your share in
a life beyond the skies

burying the talent that is ours

you use their words
to call
your sister
your brother
terrorist
learnt so well
the lesson of your conquerors
that now you, too
feel certain
you are too ignorant
to determine your destiny

so you welcome their invasions
echoing their words
you call their rape
deliverance

But water cannot run
up-hill

At dinner parties
decked with swaying palm-trees
exotic masks
from the continent
which their vision
has made dark
they swill their drink
and if you only listen
with your belly
and shut those ears
which they have created
you will hear

that there is tinkling laughter
about those whom they call
those ignorant natives
who see the conquering crows as saviours
those pliant natives
who would
sell dey mudder for penny cassava

and
the dead body shivers
the dead ash feels choked
as the vultures swoop

and my love for you
and for our land
makes their laughter burn my ears
and knot my fists
and even though tomorrow
your neighbour will shout
a silent scream of agony
in answer to your weapon's bark
even though today
we know that we must
throttle within you
the seed of malintent
planted by a greedy stranger's hand

I sing with pain
even as the anger grows
for you have learnt their evil lesson well
and I will sing yet again with pain
even beyond the silence
of your bullet's shattered fragments
for the evil lesson
must be taken from the wind

their books must stay
only
as marvel-pieces for our museum's future
and that you may rediscover our truth
and cast out that
which you now hold close as yours
that the water may flow downhill
as it must
let my song stay upon the wind.